---

(name)

---

(date started)

---

(date finished)

# The Seven Stages of Grief

I have lost many people that I love throughout my life. The most soul-crushing loss I have felt was that of my grandmother. She was so much more than a grandmother to me. She was everything. She raised me and one of my sisters. She was a grandmother, a mother, and a best friend all in one. Although it has been nearly eleven years since her passing, I still remember the moment as though it were yesterday.

It left a hole in my heart, and I fell into a depression that I never thought I could escape. Though I continue to feel the pain of loss and never go a day without thinking about her, I no longer allow that pain to paralyze me the way I once did because I know that she would not want that for me or for anyone.

Grief is a part of life. As much as we would like to be able to shield ourselves from the inevitable, we all know that it is coming. We are not meant to be on this earth forever. We will die, and so will those we love.

However, no matter how logically we look at this or how many times we tell ourselves this, we are never truly ready to let go. When we suffer a tragic loss, we go through a range of emotions so severe and so overwhelming that we feel we as though we cannot go on. How can we live without this person in our lives? How can the world just continue to go on as if nothing happened? Will we ever feel whole again? So many thoughts flood our minds and leave us with many tear-filled, sleepless nights.

However, all is not lost. One thing I have realized is that even in the darkest of moments when it feels as if the whole world is crashing down all around you, a light can be found if you just hold on to the tiniest shred of hope. You will get through this. Just take it one day at a time. Of course, no one truly expects you to simply move on and let go in only a week or even a month. That is unreasonable.

However, the seven stages of grief do not come and go on any standard timeline. You may experience one stage over the course of a day or a week or even months, or you may cycle through them all on a daily basis. Every person and every loss is different. The important thing is to understand what you are feeling and to deal with the pain without surrendering to it.

# Opening Questions

Please reflect on each question

and record your current thoughts

How many stages have you experienced since learning of the loss of a loved one?

How have you handled them?

Are you angry and resentful, depressed and withdrawn, or hopeful yet hurting?

Whatever you are feeling, just know that it is normal. You are not alone.

# DAY ONE

The first stage of grief is shock. This is perhaps the most overwhelming emotion you will feel during the initial grief process. The morning my grandmother passed away, my father woke us to tell us. We had planned to go see her in the hospital that day, but we never got the chance.

She passed away shortly after 1 am. I will never forget that moment. My dad could not even tell us. He could not find the words, but we knew. My heart felt as though it stopped. I could barely breathe. It was as if everything was falling apart. How could this happen? She had quit smoking. She was supposed to get better. She was so excited about becoming a great-grandmother again, but she would never get the chance to hold my baby in her arms. The overwhelming despair washed over me, and I felt as though I would collapse into nothingness.

As my husband held me and tried to comfort me, all I could think was that I wished it were her arms wrapped around me.

When you first get the news, it can feel as though you have had the wind knocked out of you. You may be flooded with emotions and thoughts of words left unsaid, promises not kept, or moments not shared. Perhaps you fought with them recently or have some other regrets.

**We have all been there. We all grieve, and we all have regrets.**

Whatever the case may be, you certainly are not alone. We have all been there. We all grieve, and we all have regrets. Even Jesus grieved. It is comforting to know that even someone who was so perfect and had complete knowledge of life after death, someone who had the power to bring the dead back to life still felt the same all-encompassing grief that we all feel.

When he heard of
the passing of
Lazarus, he wept.
(John 11:35)

He wept for the death of his friend. He wept for Lazarus's sisters and all the others who loved him as well. He knew he could and would bring him back to life, yet he still grieved for his beloved friend. Some feel guilty that their grief is so strong. They try to reason that their belief in life after death should grant them a serenity and an ability to move on without feeling the grief that everyone else feels. However, that is too much to ask of anyone, even yourself. The pain is real, and no matter what people want to believe you cannot just flick a switch and turn it off.

One of the hardest things in life is discovering the end of someone else's, especially someone close to you.

One of the hardest things in life is discovering the end of someone else's, especially someone close to you… whether that person is a spouse, a parent, a sibling, a child, a grandparent, or a friend. What were you doing the moment you heard the news? What thoughts and feelings did you experience? Did you have any regrets? If you do, just know that they know how you are feeling, and they understand. Everyone makes mistakes, and everyone has things they wish they had done or said. What would you say to this person if they were standing in front of you right now? Say it out loud… to yourself, to them, to God. It can be cathartic.

# Day One Questions

Please reflect on each question and record your current thoughts

What were you doing the moment you heard the news?

What thoughts and feelings did you experience?

Do you have any regrets?

# DAY TWO

The second stage of grief is denial. You begin to wonder if this is some cruel joke. No, this cannot be happening. They can't be gone. I just spoke to them. This is especially true if the person died young, and nothing is worse than the loss of a child. No parent should have to bury their child, yet they do. My grandmother suffered the loss of two of her children during her life. The first was her infant son who died from SIDS (sudden infant death syndrome). The second was her firstborn son, who died from brain cancer at the age of thirty-nine. My grandmother was so distraught that my father had to practically carry her into her house when she got home later that evening.

# All loss is difficult, and no one is immune.

All loss is difficult, and no one is immune. You long to have that person back. You think back on your memories together and try to tell yourself this is all a dream and that you just need to wake up. Unfortunately, no amount of pinching will bring back your loved one.

However, it can be comforting to know that they are no longer suffering. They no longer feel sickness or pain. They are happy.

They are in the best place they possibly could be. Reminding ourselves that this is not permanent and that we will see them again someday can help us to achieve an inner peace that otherwise would not be easily attained.

# Day Two Questions

Please reflect on each question
and record your current thoughts

In what way has denial taken over your life since losing your loved one?

Do you have a friend or family member to whom you can turn for comfort and guidance?

Often, dealing with grief becomes easier when we are in the company of those who are also experiencing these feelings.

# DAY THREE

The third stage of grief is anger. When you have come to realize that this is not a cruel dream or a horrific nightmare and that your loved one is not coming back, feelings or shock and sadness give way to resentment and anger. People experiencing this stage of grief become angry at the world, at the situation, at God, and often even at the person they are grieving. Why did you have to take them from me, God? Why, (insert name of beloved here), were you not more careful? Or why did you not go to the doctor? Why do these things always happen to good people? We become angry, and we want answers from somebody, anybody. We want someone to blame. We want to make sense of the senseless. It is a dark state of mind, yet it is a necessary one.

Suppressing these feelings will not help anything. Until we have properly dealt with all our thoughts and feelings, we can never hope to move on with our lives. Each stage has its purpose and helps to reveal something that will allow us to cope.

If we try to resist rather than dealing with the anger, we will never get over it. It will stew inside of us until we either boil over or lose ourselves. We can become drained, physically and mentally. Talking with others and especially with God can help tremendously. Try writing down your feelings.

# Day Three Questions

Please reflect on each question and record your current thoughts

In what ways have you found yourself growing angry?

With whom are you angry?

Why are you angry?

Are you angry because the death was caused by carelessness or tragedy or disease?

## Today's Challenge:

Be proactive. Share the story and ensure that the person did not die in vain and that others do not experience the same loss.

It will help you to let go, and it will allow their legacy to live on. It will give their death purpose, which can be an incredible thing.

In what ways could the loss of your loved one help others?

Would fulfilling their projects or passions also bring purpose and meaning to your life?

# DAY FOUR

The fourth stage of grief is bargaining. Often while grieving, we begin to bargain. If God brings the person back or ends our suffering, we will be better people. We will go to church every week, and we will give double... no, triple what we usually give. We will help others and be the best that we can every day of our lives.

Sometimes, we'll wish that we were the ones who died rather than them.

Please, God, take me instead! We will beg and plead for one more chance. We will beg for the opportunity to see this person just one more time, to hear their voice and tell them how much we love them. We cry out, hoping beyond hope that there is something, anything we can do to bring them back or otherwise end the pain that we are feeling.

Have you felt these emotions yet? Have you been bargaining with God, the universe, and anyone who will listen? Have you wondered what it would take to bring them back? Have you made promise after promise in the hopes that God will grant you a miracle? Sadly, miracles do not always happen the way we'd hope. That does not mean that they do not exist or that we are not loved or that our pain does not matter. It just means that it is not meant to be. Sometimes bad things happen to make way for good things. Perhaps this person fulfilled their destiny on earth and/or was meant for bigger and better things in the great beyond. Perhaps their death was meant to bring life to others. Everyone and everything has a purpose, even death.

# Day Four Questions

Please reflect on each question and record your current thoughts

Have you felt these emotions yet? Have you been bargaining with God, the universe, and anyone who will listen?

Have you wondered what it would take to bring them back?

Have you made promise after promise in the hopes that God will grant you a miracle?

# DAY FIVE

The fifth stage of grief is depression. This is the most obvious stage and perhaps the longest and most recurring as well. When we realize the inevitable and begin to give up, we start to lose hope. We stop denying what has happened. We stop bargaining. We give up. We fall deep into despair. Nights are spent sobbing into our pillows, unable to find the sleep we so desperately seek. Like Jacob*, we can be completely inconsolable. Nothing anyone can do or say will help.

Reflect on what you have been feeling lately. Have you begun to feel hopeless and lost? Have you stopped going out or talking about your feelings? Have you given up? Perhaps you have even stopped enjoying the things you used to love. Hobbies no longer bring you joy. Nothing does. Memories of your loved one leave a knot in your stomach that brings you to your knees. We have all been there. It is a terrible feeling, but it is not easily overcome. It will take some time. Talk things out with those you love. Reach out to others for help. Do not deal with this alone. Some alone time can certainly be good for you, but too much can cause you to fall into a pit of loneliness and despair that will completely overcome you and wipe out any remaining joy you may have. Feel the pain and deal with it, but please do not let it take any more from you. Be strong. You can get through this.

And Jacob rent his clothes, and put sackcloth upon his loins, and mourned for his son many days. And all his sons and all his daughters rose up to comfort him; but he refused to be comforted; and he said, For I will go down into the grave unto my son mourning. Thus his father wept for him.

Genesis 37:34-35

# Day Five Questions

Please reflect on each question

and record your current thoughts

Have you begun to feel hopeless and lost?

Have you stopped going out or talking about your feelings?

Do you feel like you given up?

Be strong. You will get through this.

# DAY SIX

The sixth stage of grief is testing. When you begin to realize that you cannot dwell on your loss and pain forever and that life in a deep, dark pit of despair is no life at all, you start trying to find ways to climb out. You search for ways to move on, ways to make sense of what has happened, and ways to give meaning to this person's death and help them or at least their legacy live on. People in this stage begin to test various ideas to see if they will alleviate the pain. Maybe getting out of the house will help. I could go out for a run or hang out with friends or family. Maybe I will go out for a spa day. Pampering might make me feel better. Or maybe playing this game or watching a movie will take my mind off things for a while. They will try anything and everything they can to make things better. This can be constructive as long as they do not get carried away. Going out, engaging with others, and doing something worthwhile can help.

What ideas can you come up with to help you move on? What hobbies can you discover? How can you take what you feel and what you have learned in order to do some good for yourself and for others? Sometimes stepping out of ourselves and focusing on others can help. Sometimes getting out and once again enjoying the things we once loved can help. Perhaps reflecting on happy memories with the person you loved and lost will bring you joy. You could do some of the things this person loved or always wanted to do in their honor... whatever it takes to connect with them and allow yourself to move on.

# Day Six Questions

Please reflect on each question

and record your current thoughts

What ideas can you come up with to help you move on?

What hobbies can you discover?

How can you take what you feel and what you have learned in order to do some good for yourself and for others?

# DAY SEVEN

The final stage of grief is acceptance. We may not have the answers we seek right now, but we can find solace in the fact that we are not alone and that everything does indeed have a purpose. The Bible says,

"To everything there is a season, and a time to every purpose under the heaven: A time to be born, and a time to die… A time to weep, and a time to laugh; a time to mourn, and a time to dance…" (Ecclesiastes 3:1-4)

Think about this and write down your

thoughts and feelings on the topic of grief and bargaining. Has it opened your eyes to anything? Is there anything you can learn from this experience? Is there a way that you can use what has happened to help others?

Perhaps you can share your experience with people who are also grieving so that you can help one another move on, or perhaps your loved one's death can serve as a warning or light a fire under researchers to help find a cure for a disease? Whatever the circumstances surrounding the person's death, there is some good that can come from it.

Find the good.

When you have finally accepted the loss, you can begin to truly move on and let go once and for all. It will still be difficult. You have a long road ahead of you. There will be times when you will lie awake at night, sobbing into your pillow. There will be times when something somewhere will remind you of them. You will never forget them, and that is a good thing. All memories are not painful.

You can have incredible memories that bring a smile to your face. You can find joy in the sights and smells that remind you of your loved one. You can move on and let them go without letting all of them go. Keep them in your heart and mind forever. Be thankful for the time that you had with them, the lessons they taught you, and the knowledge that you will see them again. You will, and it will be glorious.

# Day Seven Questions

Has it opened your eyes to anything?

Is there anything you can learn from this experience?

Is there a way that you can use what has happened to help others?

# Grief Journal

______________________________

(name)

______________________________

(date started)

______________________________

(date ended)

# Month 1

"Blessed are those
who mourn,
for they will be
comforted."
– Matthew 5:4

Today's mood:

| Positives: | Negatives: |
| --- | --- |
| | |

Today I am thankful for:

Today I learned:

Entry:

✝ Today's mood:

| Positives: | Negatives: |
|---|---|
| ______________________ | ______________________ |
| ______________________ | ______________________ |
| ______________________ | ______________________ |
| ______________________ | ______________________ |
| ______________________ | ______________________ |

Today I am thankful for: ______________________

Today I learned: ______________________

______________________

______________________

______________________

______________________

Entry: ______________________

______________________

______________________

______________________

______________________

______________________

______________________

______________________

______________________

______________________

______________________

✝ Today's mood:

| Positives: | Negatives: |
|---|---|
| ______ | ______ |
| ______ | ______ |
| ______ | ______ |
| ______ | ______ |
| ______ | ______ |

Today I am thankful for: ______

Today I learned: ______

Entry: ______

✞ Today's mood:

| Positives: | Negatives: |
| --- | --- |
| ______ | ______ |
| ______ | ______ |
| ______ | ______ |
| ______ | ______ |
| ______ | ______ |

Today I am thankful for: ______

Today I learned: ______

______

______

______

______

Entry: ______

______

______

______

______

______

______

______

______

______

______

✝ Today's mood:

| Positives: | Negatives: |
|---|---|
| | |

Today I am thankful for:

Today I learned:

Entry:

✞ Today's mood:

| Positives: | Negatives: |
| --- | --- |
| | |

Today I am thankful for: __________

Today I learned: __________

Entry: __________

✝ Today's mood:

| Positives: | Negatives: |
| --- | --- |
| | |

Today I am thankful for:

Today I learned:

Entry:

✞ Today's mood:

| Positives: | Negatives: |
| --- | --- |
| ____________________ | ____________________ |
| ____________________ | ____________________ |
| ____________________ | ____________________ |
| ____________________ | ____________________ |
| ____________________ | ____________________ |

Today I am thankful for: ____________________

Today I learned: ____________________

____________________

____________________

____________________

____________________

Entry: ____________________

____________________

____________________

____________________

____________________

____________________

____________________

____________________

____________________

____________________

____________________

✝ Today's mood:

| Positives: | Negatives: |
| --- | --- |
| | |

Today I am thankful for:

Today I learned:

Entry:

✞ Today's mood:

| Positives: | Negatives: |
| --- | --- |
| | |

Today I am thankful for:

Today I learned:

Entry:

✝ Today's mood:

| Positives: | Negatives: |
|---|---|
| ______________________ | ______________________ |
| ______________________ | ______________________ |
| ______________________ | ______________________ |
| ______________________ | ______________________ |
| ______________________ | ______________________ |

Today I am thankful for: ______________________

Today I learned: ______________________

Entry: ______________________

✝ Today's mood:

| Positives: | Negatives: |
| --- | --- |
| | |

Today I am thankful for: ______

Today I learned: ______

Entry: ______

✝ Today's mood:

| Positives: | Negatives: |
| --- | --- |
| | |

Today I am thankful for:

Today I learned:

Entry:

✝ Today's mood:

| Positives: | Negatives: |
| --- | --- |
| ______________________ | ______________________ |
| ______________________ | ______________________ |
| ______________________ | ______________________ |
| ______________________ | ______________________ |
| ______________________ | ______________________ |

Today I am thankful for: ______________________

Today I learned: ______________________

______________________

______________________

______________________

______________________

Entry: ______________________

______________________

______________________

______________________

______________________

______________________

______________________

______________________

______________________

______________________

______________________

✞ Today's mood:

| Positives: | Negatives: |
| --- | --- |
| ______ | ______ |
| ______ | ______ |
| ______ | ______ |
| ______ | ______ |
| ______ | ______ |

Today I am thankful for: ______

Today I learned: ______

Entry: ______

✝ Today's mood:

| Positives: | Negatives: |
| --- | --- |
| | |

Today I am thankful for:

Today I learned:

Entry:

✞ Today's mood:

| Positives: | Negatives: |
|---|---|
| | |

Today I am thankful for:

Today I learned:

Entry:

✞ Today's mood:

| Positives: | Negatives: |
| --- | --- |
| | |

Today I am thankful for:

Today I learned:

Entry:

✝ Today's mood:

| Positives: | Negatives: |
| --- | --- |
| | |

Today I am thankful for: ______________________________

Today I learned: ______________________________

Entry: ______________________________

✞ Today's mood:

| Positives: | Negatives: |
| --- | --- |
| ______________________________ | ______________________________ |
| ______________________________ | ______________________________ |
| ______________________________ | ______________________________ |
| ______________________________ | ______________________________ |
| ______________________________ | ______________________________ |

Today I am thankful for: ______________________________

Today I learned: ______________________________

______________________________

______________________________

______________________________

______________________________

Entry: ______________________________

______________________________

______________________________

______________________________

______________________________

______________________________

______________________________

______________________________

______________________________

______________________________

______________________________

✝ Today's mood:

| Positives: | Negatives: |
|---|---|
| | |

Today I am thankful for:

Today I learned:

Entry:

✝ Today's mood:

| Positives: | Negatives: |
| --- | --- |
| | |

Today I am thankful for:

Today I learned:

Entry:

✝ Today's mood:

| Positives: | Negatives: |
| --- | --- |
| | |

Today I am thankful for:

Today I learned:

Entry:

✝ Today's mood:

| Positives: | Negatives: |
| --- | --- |
| | |

Today I am thankful for: ______

Today I learned: ______

Entry: ______

✝ Today's mood:

| Positives: | Negatives: |
| --- | --- |
| | |

Today I am thankful for:

Today I learned:

Entry:

✞ Today's mood:

| Positives: | Negatives: |
| --- | --- |
| | |

Today I am thankful for:

Today I learned:

Entry:

✝ Today's mood:

| Positives: | Negatives: |
| --- | --- |
| | |

Today I am thankful for:

Today I learned:

Entry:

✞ Today's mood:

| Positives: | Negatives: |
| --- | --- |
| | |

Today I am thankful for:

Today I learned:

Entry:

✝ Today's mood:

| Positives: | Negatives: |
| --- | --- |
| | |

Today I am thankful for:

Today I learned:

Entry:

✞ Today's mood:

| Positives: | Negatives: |
| --- | --- |
| | |

Today I am thankful for:

Today I learned:

Entry:

# Month 2

"You, Lord, keep my lamp burning; my God turns my darkness into light."

– Psalm 18:28

✝ Today's mood:

| Positives: | Negatives: |
| --- | --- |

Today I am thankful for:

Today I learned:

Entry:

✝ Today's mood:

| Positives: | Negatives: |
| --- | --- |
| ______________________ | ______________________ |
| ______________________ | ______________________ |
| ______________________ | ______________________ |
| ______________________ | ______________________ |
| ______________________ | ______________________ |

Today I am thankful for: ______________________

Today I learned: ______________________

______________________

______________________

______________________

______________________

Entry: ______________________

______________________

______________________

______________________

______________________

______________________

______________________

______________________

______________________

______________________

______________________

✝ Today's mood:

| Positives: | Negatives: |
|---|---|
| | |

Today I am thankful for:

Today I learned:

Entry:

✝ Today's mood:

| Positives: | Negatives: |
|---|---|
| | |

Today I am thankful for:

Today I learned:

Entry:

✝ Today's mood:

| Positives: | Negatives: |
| --- | --- |
| | |

Today I am thankful for:

Today I learned:

Entry:

✝ Today's mood:

| Positives: | Negatives: |
| --- | --- |
| ______________________ | ______________________ |
| ______________________ | ______________________ |
| ______________________ | ______________________ |
| ______________________ | ______________________ |
| ______________________ | ______________________ |

Today I am thankful for: ______________________________

Today I learned: ______________________________

______________________________________________

______________________________________________

______________________________________________

______________________________________________

Entry: ______________________________________

______________________________________________

______________________________________________

______________________________________________

______________________________________________

______________________________________________

______________________________________________

______________________________________________

______________________________________________

______________________________________________

______________________________________________

✝ Today's mood:

| Positives: | Negatives: |
| --- | --- |
| | |

Today I am thankful for:

Today I learned:

Entry:

✝ Today's mood:

| Positives: | Negatives: |
| --- | --- |
| | |

Today I am thankful for:

Today I learned:

Entry:

✝ Today's mood:

| Positives: | Negatives: |
| --- | --- |
| | |

Today I am thankful for:

Today I learned:

Entry:

Today's mood:

| Positives: | Negatives: |
|---|---|
| | |

Today I am thankful for:

Today I learned:

Entry:

✞ Today's mood:

| Positives: | Negatives: |
| --- | --- |
| ___ | ___ |
| ___ | ___ |
| ___ | ___ |
| ___ | ___ |
| ___ | ___ |

Today I am thankful for: ___

Today I learned: ___

___

___

___

___

Entry: ___

___

___

___

___

___

___

___

___

___

___

✝ Today's mood:

| Positives: | Negatives: |
| --- | --- |
| | |

Today I am thankful for: ______________________

Today I learned: ______________________

Entry: ______________________

✝ Today's mood:

| Positives: | Negatives: |
| --- | --- |
| | |

Today I am thankful for:

Today I learned:

Entry:

✝ Today's mood:

| Positives: | Negatives: |
| --- | --- |
| | |

Today I am thankful for:

Today I learned:

Entry:

✝ Today's mood:

| Positives: | Negatives: |
| --- | --- |
| ______________________ | ______________________ |
| ______________________ | ______________________ |
| ______________________ | ______________________ |
| ______________________ | ______________________ |
| ______________________ | ______________________ |

Today I am thankful for: ______________________

Today I learned: ______________________

______________________

______________________

______________________

______________________

Entry: ______________________

______________________

______________________

______________________

______________________

______________________

______________________

______________________

______________________

______________________

______________________

Today's mood:

| Positives: | Negatives: |
|---|---|
| | |

Today I am thankful for:

Today I learned:

Entry:

✝ Today's mood:

| Positives: | Negatives: |
| --- | --- |
| | |

Today I am thankful for:

Today I learned:

Entry:

✞ Today's mood:

| Positives: | Negatives: |
| --- | --- |
| | |

Today I am thankful for:

Today I learned:

Entry:

✝ Today's mood:

| Positives: | Negatives: |
|---|---|
| | |

Today I am thankful for:

Today I learned:

Entry:

✝ Today's mood:

| Positives: | Negatives: |
| --- | --- |
| | |

Today I am thankful for:

Today I learned:

Entry:

✝ Today's mood:

| Positives: | Negatives: |
| --- | --- |
| | |

Today I am thankful for:

Today I learned:

Entry:

Today's mood:

| Positives: | Negatives: |
| --- | --- |
| | |

Today I am thankful for:

Today I learned:

Entry:

✝ Today's mood:

| Positives: | Negatives: |
| --- | --- |
| | |

Today I am thankful for:

Today I learned:

Entry:

✝ Today's mood:

| Positives: | Negatives: |
|---|---|
| | |

Today I am thankful for: __________

Today I learned: __________

Entry: __________

✞ Today's mood:

| Positives: | Negatives: |
| --- | --- |
| | |

Today I am thankful for:

Today I learned:

Entry:

✝ Today's mood:

| Positives: | Negatives: |
|---|---|
| ______________________ | ______________________ |
| ______________________ | ______________________ |
| ______________________ | ______________________ |
| ______________________ | ______________________ |
| ______________________ | ______________________ |

Today I am thankful for: ______________________

Today I learned: ______________________

Entry: ______________________

✝ Today's mood:

| Positives: | Negatives: |
| --- | --- |
| | |

Today I am thankful for:

Today I learned:

Entry:

✝ Today's mood:

| Positives: | Negatives: |
| --- | --- |
| ______ | ______ |
| ______ | ______ |
| ______ | ______ |
| ______ | ______ |
| ______ | ______ |

Today I am thankful for: ______

Today I learned: ______

Entry: ______

✝ Today's mood:

| Positives: | Negatives: |
| --- | --- |
| ______ | ______ |
| ______ | ______ |
| ______ | ______ |
| ______ | ______ |
| ______ | ______ |

Today I am thankful for: ______

Today I learned: ______

Entry: ______

✝ Today's mood:

| Positives: | Negatives: |
| --- | --- |
| | |

Today I am thankful for:

Today I learned:

Entry:

# Month 3

"My comfort in my suffering is this: Your promise preserves my life."

– Psalm 119:50

✝ Today's mood:

| Positives: | Negatives: |
| --- | --- |
| | |

Today I am thankful for:

Today I learned:

Entry:

✝ Today's mood:

| Positives: | Negatives: |
| --- | --- |
| | |

Today I am thankful for:

Today I learned:

Entry:

✝ Today's mood:

| Positives: | Negatives: |
| --- | --- |
| | |

Today I am thankful for:

Today I learned:

Entry:

✝ Today's mood:

| Positives: | Negatives: |
| --- | --- |
| | |
| | |
| | |
| | |
| | |

Today I am thankful for:

Today I learned:

Entry:

✝ Today's mood:

| Positives: | Negatives: |
| --- | --- |
| | |

Today I am thankful for: ______________________

Today I learned: ______________________

Entry: ______________________

✝ Today's mood:

| Positives: | Negatives: |
|---|---|
| | |

Today I am thankful for:

Today I learned:

Entry:

✝ Today's mood:

| Positives: | Negatives: |
|---|---|
| | |

Today I am thankful for:

Today I learned:

Entry:

✝ Today's mood:

| Positives: | Negatives: |
| --- | --- |
| | |

Today I am thankful for:

Today I learned:

Entry:

✝ Today's mood:

| Positives: | Negatives: |
| --- | --- |
| | |

Today I am thankful for:

Today I learned:

Entry:

✞ Today's mood:

| Positives: | Negatives: |
| --- | --- |
| ______ | ______ |
| ______ | ______ |
| ______ | ______ |
| ______ | ______ |
| ______ | ______ |

Today I am thankful for: ______

Today I learned: ______

Entry: ______

✞ Today's mood:

| Positives: | Negatives: |
| --- | --- |
| ____________ | ____________ |
| ____________ | ____________ |
| ____________ | ____________ |
| ____________ | ____________ |
| ____________ | ____________ |

Today I am thankful for: ____________

Today I learned: ____________

Entry: ____________

✝ Today's mood:

| Positives: | Negatives: |
| --- | --- |
| ______________________ | ______________________ |
| ______________________ | ______________________ |
| ______________________ | ______________________ |
| ______________________ | ______________________ |
| ______________________ | ______________________ |

Today I am thankful for: ______________________

Today I learned: ______________________

______________________

______________________

______________________

______________________

Entry: ______________________

______________________

______________________

______________________

______________________

______________________

______________________

______________________

______________________

______________________

______________________

✝ Today's mood:

| Positives: | Negatives: |
| --- | --- |
| ________________________ | ________________________ |
| ________________________ | ________________________ |
| ________________________ | ________________________ |
| ________________________ | ________________________ |
| ________________________ | ________________________ |

Today I am thankful for: ________________________

Today I learned: ________________________

________________________

________________________

________________________

________________________

Entry: ________________________

________________________

________________________

________________________

________________________

________________________

________________________

________________________

________________________

________________________

________________________

✝ Today's mood:

| Positives: | Negatives: |
| --- | --- |
| | |

Today I am thankful for:

Today I learned:

Entry:

✝ Today's mood:

| Positives: | Negatives: |
| --- | --- |
| | |

Today I am thankful for:

Today I learned:

Entry:

✝ Today's mood:

| Positives: | Negatives: |
| --- | --- |
| | |

Today I am thankful for:

Today I learned:

Entry:

✝ Today's mood:

| Positives: | Negatives: |
| --- | --- |
| ______________ | ______________ |
| ______________ | ______________ |
| ______________ | ______________ |
| ______________ | ______________ |
| ______________ | ______________ |

Today I am thankful for: ______________________________

Today I learned: ______________________________

______________________________

______________________________

______________________________

______________________________

Entry: ______________________________

______________________________

______________________________

______________________________

______________________________

______________________________

______________________________

______________________________

______________________________

______________________________

______________________________

✝ Today's mood:

| Positives: | Negatives: |
| --- | --- |
| | |

Today I am thankful for:

Today I learned:

Entry:

✝ Today's mood:

| Positives: | Negatives: |
| --- | --- |
| | |

Today I am thankful for:

Today I learned:

Entry:

✝ Today's mood:

| Positives: | Negatives: |
| --- | --- |
| ____________________ | ____________________ |
| ____________________ | ____________________ |
| ____________________ | ____________________ |
| ____________________ | ____________________ |
| ____________________ | ____________________ |

Today I am thankful for: ____________________

Today I learned: ____________________

____________________

____________________

____________________

____________________

Entry: ____________________

____________________

____________________

____________________

____________________

____________________

____________________

____________________

____________________

____________________

____________________

✝ Today's mood:

| Positives: | Negatives: |
|---|---|
| ______________________ | ______________________ |
| ______________________ | ______________________ |
| ______________________ | ______________________ |
| ______________________ | ______________________ |
| ______________________ | ______________________ |

Today I am thankful for: ______________________

Today I learned: ______________________

______________________

______________________

______________________

______________________

Entry: ______________________

______________________

______________________

______________________

______________________

______________________

______________________

______________________

______________________

______________________

______________________

✝ Today's mood:

| Positives: | Negatives: |
| --- | --- |
| ______________________________ | ______________________________ |
| ______________________________ | ______________________________ |
| ______________________________ | ______________________________ |
| ______________________________ | ______________________________ |
| ______________________________ | ______________________________ |

Today I am thankful for: ______________________________

Today I learned: ______________________________

______________________________________________

______________________________________________

______________________________________________

______________________________________________

Entry: ______________________________________________

______________________________________________

______________________________________________

______________________________________________

______________________________________________

______________________________________________

______________________________________________

______________________________________________

______________________________________________

______________________________________________

______________________________________________

✝ Today's mood:

| Positives: | Negatives: |
| --- | --- |
| ______ | ______ |
| ______ | ______ |
| ______ | ______ |
| ______ | ______ |
| ______ | ______ |

Today I am thankful for: ______

Today I learned: ______

______

______

______

______

Entry: ______

______

______

______

______

______

______

______

______

______

______

✝ Today's mood:

| Positives: | Negatives: |
| --- | --- |
| ______________________ | ______________________ |
| ______________________ | ______________________ |
| ______________________ | ______________________ |
| ______________________ | ______________________ |
| ______________________ | ______________________ |

Today I am thankful for: ______________________

Today I learned: ______________________

______________________

______________________

______________________

______________________

Entry: ______________________

______________________

______________________

______________________

______________________

______________________

______________________

______________________

______________________

______________________

______________________

✝ Today's mood:

| Positives: | Negatives: |
| --- | --- |
| | |

Today I am thankful for:

Today I learned:

Entry:

✝ Today's mood:

| Positives: | Negatives: |
| --- | --- |
| ______________ | ______________ |
| ______________ | ______________ |
| ______________ | ______________ |
| ______________ | ______________ |
| ______________ | ______________ |

Today I am thankful for: ______________

Today I learned: ______________

______________

______________

______________

______________

Entry: ______________

______________

______________

______________

______________

______________

______________

______________

______________

______________

______________

✝ Today's mood:

| Positives: | Negatives: |
| --- | --- |
| ______ | ______ |
| ______ | ______ |
| ______ | ______ |
| ______ | ______ |
| ______ | ______ |

Today I am thankful for: ______

Today I learned: ______

Entry: ______

✝ Today's mood:

| Positives: | Negatives: |
| --- | --- |
| | |

Today I am thankful for:

Today I learned:

Entry:

✝ Today's mood:

| Positives: | Negatives: |
| --- | --- |
| ______________ | ______________ |
| ______________ | ______________ |
| ______________ | ______________ |
| ______________ | ______________ |
| ______________ | ______________ |

Today I am thankful for: ______________

Today I learned: ______________

______________

______________

______________

______________

Entry: ______________

______________

______________

______________

______________

______________

______________

______________

______________

______________

______________

Made in the USA
Coppell, TX
09 December 2020

43995709R00128